SHEE

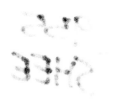

Growing Up in
Iran

Other titles in the *Growing Up Around the World* series include:

Growing Up in
Iran

Barbara Sheen

ReferencePoint
Press®

San Diego, CA

For more information, contact:
ReferencePoint Press, Inc.
PO Box 27779
San Diego, CA 92198
www.ReferencePointPress.com

LIBRARY OF CONGRESS CATALOGING-IN-PUBLICATION DATA

Name: Sheen, Barbara, author.
Title: Growing Up in Iran/by Barbara Sheen.
Description: San Diego, CA: Reference Point Press, 2018. | Series: Growing
  Up Around the World series | Includes bibliographical references and index.
Identifiers: LCCN 2017011707 (print) | LCCN 2017013207 (ebook) | ISBN
  9781682822166 (eBook) | ISBN 9781682822159 (hardcover)
Subjects: LCSH: Iran—Social life and customs. | Iran—Religious life and customs.
Classification: LCC DS266 (ebook) | LCC DS266 .S5856 2018 (print) | DDC
  955--dc23
LC record available at https://lccn.loc.gov/2017011707

CONTENTS

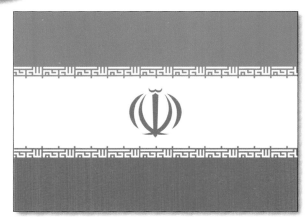

Official Name
Islamic Republic of Iran

Size
636,371 sq. miles
(1,648,193 sq. km)

Total Population
82,801,633 as of 2016

Youth Population
0–14 years: 23.65%
15–24 years: 16.57%

Religion
Muslim: 99.4%
Other (Christian, Jewish,
Zoroastrian): 0.3%
Unspecified: 0.4%

Capital
Tehran

Type of Government
Theocratic republic

Language
Persian (53%), plus other unofficial languages,
including Azerbaijani and other Turkic dialects
(18%), Kurdish (10%), Gilaki and Mazandarani
(7%), Luri (6%), Arabic (2%), and Balochi (2%)

Currency
Iranian rial

Industries
Petroleum, petrochemicals, gas, fertilizers, textiles,
cement and other construction materials, food
processing, metal fabrication, armaments

Literacy
86.8% (age 15+); 98.7% (age 15–24)

Internet Users
36.07 million, or 44.1% of population
as of 2015

CHAPTER ONE

A Complex Nation

Iran is a complex, multifaceted nation that cannot easily be categorized. It is a country of snow-capped mountains and arid deserts; of ancient ruins and modern high-rise apartment buildings. It is home to beautiful domed mosques, as well as Christian, Jewish, and Zoroastrian houses of worship. It has bustling cities where billboards advertising fast food and designer boutiques hang near murals glorifying the nation's supreme leader. It contains nuclear power plants, offshore oil rigs, and tranquil rural villages. It is a nation where hospitality is an important part of local culture and visitors are always welcome.

It is also a nation where civil and religious laws are one, where women are required to cover their heads and bodies in public, and men can be arrested for sporting a tattoo. As Nahid, a female college student, explains, "I'm . . . tired of having to worry every two seconds on the streets that I'm going to get stopped or arrested for my hair sticking out of my scarf or my butt sticking out from underneath my overcoat!"[1]

Iran is, indeed, a complex nation. The many layers that make up this nation affect the lives of the young people growing up here.

Diverse Geography

Iran is a large, geographically diverse country located in the Middle East. It is bordered by Armenia, Azerbaijan, Turkmenistan, and the Caspian Sea in the north; the Persian Gulf and the Gulf of Oman in the south; Afghanistan and Pakistan in the east; and Iraq and Turkey in the west. Covering an area of 636,371 square miles (1,648,193 sq. km), it is the second-largest nation in the Middle East and the eighteenth-largest nation on earth.

Iran's landscape is dominated by rugged mountains that surround a high central plateau where most of the nation's major cities are located. Vast deserts crisscross the plateau, and small flower-strewn plains can be found on both coasts.

The climate varies by region. In general, the weather is hot and dry in the summer and cold in the winter. The mountains shield much of the nation from significant rainfall. Runoff from mountain snow, which is carried to farms and villages via underground aqueducts known as *qanats*, provides most of the country's water. This system allows farmers to grow a variety of crops, including rice, wheat, fruits, and nuts.

Iran also holds the world's second-largest oil and gas reserves. It produces about 3.3 million barrels of oil per day. Moreover, Iran has large undeveloped mineral reserves, including the largest zinc reserves and second-largest copper reserves in the world.

Most of Iran's major cities, including its capital, Tehran (pictured), lie on a high plateau surrounded by rugged mountains.

Young people growing up in such a diverse nation have different experiences depending on where they live. But almost all young Iranians are proud of their nation's natural beauty, geographic diversity, and mineral wealth.

A Long and Tumultuous History

Young Iranians are also proud of and influenced by their nation's history. Iran's location at the crossroads of Asia and the Middle East has made it an important country for thousands of years. Historians believe that humans first inhabited the land that comprises Iran about one hundred thousand years ago. Formerly known as Persia, it was the home of a number of highly advanced ancient civilizations whose ruins dot modern Iran's landscape. In fact, around 500 BCE, the Persian Empire ranked as a superpower. With a national philosophy that peace comes through strength, it conquered large swathes of the world. The empire spanned three continents (Asia, Africa, and Europe) and encompassed about 40 percent of the world's population at the time. Ancient Persia also served as the center of the Silk Road, the ancient trade route that linked Asia and Europe.

Persia's status, wealth, and strategic location attracted the interest of other nations. Over the centuries, it was repeatedly conquered by different invading forces, only to repeatedly rise up and regain control before facing a new invasion. As blogger Parsa explains, "We have experienced the highs and lows of life perhaps like no other people over a long period of time. In one generation we have been held in the highest regard, only to be sold as slaves or slaughtered in the next."[2]

Among these invaders were Arab Muslims who brought Islam to Persia in the seventh century CE. Soon Islam was the dominant religion. In 1501 it was declared the national religion.

In the ensuing centuries, Persian kings, known as shahs, ruled the nation (which changed its name to Iran in 1935). When oil was discovered in 1908, British Petroleum, then known as the Anglo-Iranian Oil Company, gained control of Iran's oil fields. For the next fifty years, Great Britain earned millions of dollars from Iranian oil fields but gave Iran only a small portion of the profits. In 1951, with the shah acting largely as a figurehead, Iran held its first democratic election. In an attempt to resist foreign domination, the newly elected prime minister, Mohammad Mosaddeq, nationalized the oil industry. In response, in 1953 US and British intelligence agencies orchestrated a coup that toppled the democratically elected government, returned the oil industry to foreign hands, and empowered the shah. The event negatively impacted the way Iranians felt about the West. Even today many young Iranians mistrust foreign involvement in Iranian affairs. One teen explained, "The past times and today, they are like a tortoise and its shell. Even if you can pull them apart, it is not a good idea."[3]

For the next twenty-five years, the shah ruled with an iron fist. His lavish lifestyle, submission to foreign interests, and attempts to Westernize Iran by repressing Islamic values angered many Iranians. The Iranian Revolution of 1979 overthrew the shah. And, because the United States gave the shah a safe haven, a group of Iranian college students took over the American embassy in Tehran. They held fifty-two Americans hostage for more than one year. With the shah dethroned, the Islamic Republic of Iran was established under the leadership of Ayatollah Ruhollah Khomeini, a Muslim cleric, who was given the title of supreme leader.

The Custom of *Taarof*

The complexity of Iranian culture often confuses people of other nations. The custom of *taarof* (tah-rofe), especially, often perplexes visitors to Iran. The custom is a form of Persian etiquette and a sign of deference and respect that all young Iranians learn at an early age. Taarof requires that one person defer to another two times before coming to an agreement. For example, when a passenger asks a taxi driver how much a trip has cost, the driver will protest that he and his taxi are not worthy of such an important passenger, so there is no charge. The rider is expected to reply by complimenting the driver and the vehicle, then insist on paying. This little drama is repeated three times. The third time the driver acquiesces and asks for the actual fare, which the rider gladly pays. The same thing occurs when a host or hostess offers a guest food or drink. The guest must refuse the offer the first two times, saying that he or she is not worthy of such wonderful fare, but accept it the third time. To do otherwise is considered extremely rude.

To Westerners accustomed to more straightforward interactions, taarof might seem misleading. But for Iranians it is a way to show respect for one another by elevating others while humbling oneself.

Government

The Islamic Republic of Iran is a theocratic republic. A theocratic republic combines elements of a democracy with those of a theocracy. The latter is a form of government in which all laws are derived from a particular religion. Iran has three branches of government: executive, legislative, and judicial. Members of the first two branches are elected officials who serve for limited terms, while members of the judicial branch are appointed.

All government officials answer to an unelected cleric known as the supreme leader, who is the most powerful person in the country. He serves for life and selects his own successor. The only individuals he answers to are a group of clerics whom he appoints. As of 2016 Iran has had two supreme leaders, Ruhollah Khomeini (1979–1989) and Ali Khamenei (1989–present). Fatema, a young blogger, describes Iran's government: "We have a leader who is not chosen by election and who will not be leader just for 4 years but forever, till he is alive. There's no difference between this leader and a king or a dictator. Also, this leader is a religious one."[4]

All laws in Iran are based on the supreme leader's and other clerics' strict interpretation of Islamic doctrine. The goal is to follow the teaching of the Koran, uphold Islamic values and culture, and uproot Western influences, which the supreme leader believes corrupts youthful morals. As Ayatollah Khamenei stated in 2015, "They [the youth] are intellectually exposed to dangerous threats—the ways of corrupting them are many. . . . Today the country is not involved in the military war but it is involved in . . . the cultural wars."[5]

Laws derived from Islam, known as sharia law, affect almost every aspect of a young person's life. They span matters related to religious practices, dress, censorship, gender equality, education, career choices, social practices, and human sexuality, among other things. Individuals who break the laws face stiff penalties. Depending on the particular crime, lawbreakers can be fined, jailed, whipped, or even sentenced to death. For example, in 2014 a group of Ira-

> "They [the youth] are intellectually exposed to dangerous threats—the ways of corrupting them are many. . . . Today the country is not involved in the military war but it is involved in . . . the cultural wars."[5]
>
> —Ayatollah Ali Khamenei, supreme leader of the Islamic Republic of Iran

From the age of nine on, when in public, females must cover themselves either with a traditional full-body chador (woman on left) or at least have their head covered with a scarf and wear a loose fitting overcoat (women on right).

nian boys and girls were arrested for posting a video of themselves dancing to the song "Happy" on YouTube. They were sentenced to six months in prison (the prison term was later suspended) and ninety-one lashes with a whip. Iranian author Kaveh Basmenji explains, "Every weekday, hundreds of worried parents . . . swarm outside a building in one of the capital's streets to find out if their children are held in custody for breaking 'moral laws' of the Islamic state. Just in case, they come with ready cash and their own real estate deeds . . . with which to bail out their children."[6]

Indeed, many of the personal freedoms that Western teens take for granted are restricted in Iran. For example, from the age of nine, females are required to cover their heads and bodies in public. Some wear a chador, a tentlike garment that covers the wearer from head to toe. Others cover their heads with a *hijab* or scarf, and their bodies with a loose fitting coat. Other laws segregate boys from girls in schools and public places, as well as

Iranian Bazaars

Iran's cities are home to huge mazelike shopping complexes known as bazaars, where crowds of shoppers, including many teens, wander for hours. The bazaars are like cities within a city. They contain thousands of shops that sell everything imaginable. Many also contain banks, guesthouses, and mosques. Author Jamie Maslin describes the bazaar in the city of Tabriz:

> The bazaar in Tabriz is massive, totaling 2.1 miles in length and containing 7,350 shops. . . . It dates back a thousand years, although most of the buildings currently there are from the fifteenth century. The inside of the bazaar made the streets outside seem empty and quiet. There were people everywhere trying to strike a deal, browsing, feeling the quality of the goods, eating, drinking, smelling foods, working, chatting, and generally shopping until they dropped in this atmospheric labyrinth. The bazaar was separated into five main areas specializing in gold, footwear, spices, general household items, and carpets. As well as the main sections, there was . . . a section specializing in copperware and foods. . . . I couldn't help but walk around google-eyed. There were huge blocks of sugar being broken into manageable pieces, mounds of brightly colored spices and dried foodstuffs, carpets being made and mended, breads being cooked, and many, many other intriguing sights and smells. But most impressive of all was the size of the place—it went on and on forever.

Jamie Maslin, *Iranian Rappers and Persian Porn.* New York: Skyhorse, 2009, p. 57.

prohibit boys and girls from socializing with each other. Actions as seemingly trivial as boys and girls holding hands are forbidden. So are all forms of media that the government believes are contrary to Islamic values. These include, but are not limited to, certain websites, books, periodicals, and movies.

A Young Population

Iran has one of the youngest populations in the world. As of 2016 the population of Iran was 82,801,633. Of these individuals, about 40 percent were under twenty-five years old, and about 60 percent of Iranians were under thirty years old. Ethnically, most identify as Persian. Other ethnic groups include the Azeris, Kurds, Baluchis, Turkmens, and Lurs, among others. Almost all Iranians' primary language is Farsi, the name for the Persian language. About half the population also speaks an ethnic dialect.

Iranian youths have lived all of their lives under sharia law. As with any large group, they have differing opinions about their government and the laws they must follow. Some young Iranians embrace sharia law as part of their faith. Many of these boys and girls join the Basij, a voluntary paramilitary group that has many duties, including morals policing. As a Basiji explains, "I grew up in a religious family. . . . It made me want to have Basij responsibilities. I loved Islam, I loved the supreme jurisprudence. . . . It's ordinary people who join the Basij. . . . Their activities with the Basij are driven by their own desire, out of love."[7]

Other teens believe that their nation's laws are repressive and secretly disobey them. Teenage Anahita falls into this group. She explains, "We can see on satellite TV how free and happy the youth are in other countries. But look at us: we can't dress the way we like; we can't listen to music we like; we can't talk to a boy without fear of being harassed or arrested. We're all the time told what's good and what's bad. And we do the opposite!"[8]

> "Every weekday, hundreds of worried parents . . . swarm outside a building in one of the capital's streets to find out if their children are held in custody for breaking 'moral laws' of the Islamic state."[6]
>
> —Kaveh Basmenji, an Iranian journalist and author

Still other young people are political activists. These youngsters want their nation's laws to represent a compromise between Islamic beliefs and modern culture. Even though they face persecution for their actions, some of these teens participate in demonstrations supporting their beliefs.

These differing viewpoints sometimes cause divisions between Iranian youth as well as among family members. As Hamid-Reza Jalaipour, a professor at Tehran University, explains:

It's difficult to explain some aspects of what's going on with youth, because it's a new phenomenon in Iran. . . . There is a big diversity: there is religious youth, there is ideological youth, modern youth and postmodern youth who live as if they were in California. . . . They don't live according to what their parents want; they do what they want. Even the women make decisions on their own.[9]

Cities and Towns

About 73 percent of Iran's population lives in urban areas, and this number is growing as more and more young people relocate to the cities to study or work. With a population of about 8.42 million people, the nation's capital, Tehran, is the most populous city in the nation. As of 2016 the mean age of the population in Tehran was thirty-one. Other Iranian cities with at least 1 million residents include Mashhad, Esfahan, Karaj, Shiraz, and Tabriz.

Iranian cities are bustling, noisy places. Huge murals and posters promoting the supreme leader, shia Islam, and anti-American and anti-Israeli propaganda decorate the walls of tall buildings and the girders of highway overpasses. The sidewalks teem with pedestrians rushing to and fro. Despite their rush, many individuals stop to drop money into religious offering boxes located on most street corners. Unlike in Western cities, where males and females commonly intermingle, it is rare to see mixed-gender groups walking together or sitting together on benches. Even public transportation is segregated by gender; males age fifteen and up and females age nine and up are allotted separate sections of buses and train cars.

Out on the streets, motor vehicles weave and dodge every which way, not heeding traffic signals or yielding to pedestrians. Not even the sidewalks are safe. Motorcycles and mopeds often hop onto them, zigzagging around pedestrians. According to author Jared Cohen, "The traffic is atrocious, bumper-to-bumper at all moments of the day. Cars drive on whatever part of the road offers space, and it is not uncommon to see vehicles of various shapes and sizes driving on the wrong side of the road."[10]

All this traffic pollutes the air. Clouds of black smoke hover overhead, causing health issues for vulnerable individuals such as children with asthma. Tehran ranks among the top five cities that are most polluted by sulfur dioxide in the world. "The air was so filthy you might as well have been pressing your lips to the exhaust pipe of the ubiquitous pickup truck,"[11] author Nicholas Jubber recalls.

Despite these drawbacks, big-city life has a lot to offer young Iranians. There are leafy green parks, beautiful mosques and religious shrines, elegant restaurants and cozy cafés, multiplex movie theaters, museums and art galleries, libraries, universities, and sports complexes. Young shoppers flock to ultramodern malls

16

Traffic in Iran is notoriously heavy and erratic, and motorbikes often will drive up onto sidewalks, weaving around pedestrians, in order to make headway in traffic jams.

offering all sorts of chic designer goods, as well as huge maze-like bazaars offering every imaginable product—from handcrafted jewelry to freshly baked bread.

Iranian towns and villages are more peaceful places. The air, especially in mountain villages, is crystal clear, and the loudest sounds one hears are the daily calls to prayer emanating from the local mosque and the tinkling of the bells worn by goats and sheep. Were it not for the electrical wires and satellite dishes, visitors might think they had stepped back in time. Youngsters growing up in Iran's rural areas are typically less sophisticated than those growing up in the cities. Their families are often more religious than urban families. As a result, they are often more conservative in their views of the government and laws than their urban counterparts.

Looking to the Future

Like all nations, Iran faces a number of challenges as it moves into the future. One issue that concerns many young Iranians is the way they and their country are perceived by the rest of the world. Many young Iranians feel that Westerners do not understand the many facets that make up their nation. They worry that their leaders have given the outside world a negative impression of Iran, and they do not want to be judged based on the statements or actions of their government. "We are just like you," Gita, a student, says. "We are not crazy people, we are not terrorists; we are not represented by the mullahs [powerful clerics]."[12] Many of these youths feel so strongly about this issue that, at the risk of serious punishment, they author blogs aimed at helping outsiders better understand the complexity of Iranian life.

> "We are just like you. We are not crazy people, we are not terrorists; we are not represented by the mullahs."[12]
>
> —Gita, an Iranian college student

At the same time, Iranian teens remember their nation's history and its culture of peace through strength. They are wary about foreign involvement in Iran's internal affairs. Many resent other countries interfering in Iran's development of nuclear energy, which their government says will be used for clean energy but which other nations fear will be used to build nuclear weapons. No matter what the energy is used for, many Iranian teens believe that Iran has the right to develop this technology, especially if it will advance their nation's world standing. As one young woman insists, "If we want nuclear weapons why should we not be allowed to have them? America has them, China has them, . . . so many countries have them. Why can't we be the best too?"[13]

The way Iran and its people are perceived by the rest of the world, and the direction it takes in the future, rests in the hands of the nation's large youth population. Like Iran itself, Iranian youth are complex, multifaceted individuals who lead complicated lives. Although they do not always agree with each other, they want what is best for their country. Kimia, a university student in Tehran, puts it this way: "We want . . . to become a better country every day. . . . We've been through a lot of disastrous times. But I think it's our responsibility to hope."[14]

CHAPTER TWO

Home and Family

In a society in which behavior like listening to certain types of music or not observing religious rituals can get people into serious trouble, Iranians are cautious about how they behave in public and in whom they place their trust. Iranians say that they live two lives and have two distinct identities: a public identity, which is known as *zaher*, and a private identity, which is known as *batin*. Iranian youngsters learn from an early age to protect and maintain this separation. Says one teenager, "When we were six, we already knew there were two worlds: one at home and one at school. We knew that we could not talk about what went on at home with our classmates. We knew how to keep secrets. Soon, we understood who we could joke with and who we had to tell that our parents prayed 100 times a day."[15]

In public, youngsters conform to accepted roles of behavior, such as observing important religious holidays, following dress codes, and keeping their distance from members of the opposite sex. But in their homes, surrounded by their families, they can be themselves without worrying about societal rules. Teen Maryam uses the chador that she wears in public as an example of this dual existence: "I'm only wearing it because I have to. My heart wants something else entirely. The chador actually sums up the essence of Iran: underneath it, many women wear sexy lingerie—just as Iran looks Islamic on the outside, but if only you knew how things are really like underneath. All Iranians have a split personality."[16]

Iranian families support and trust each other. Home and family provide young Iranians with a safe haven where they can express themselves freely and do things like watch banned movies without worry. Home and family are the backbone of society, and trusting and helping family members is the norm.

The Nuclear Family

The majority of young Iranians grow up in a traditional nuclear family that consists of a father, mother, and siblings. The average age of marriage is twenty-two for women and twenty-seven for men. And most Iranian youngsters have at least one sibling. On average, urban couples have two children, and rural couples have three.

> "The chador actually sums up the essence of Iran: underneath it, many women wear sexy lingerie—just as Iran looks Islamic on the outside, but if only you knew how things are really like underneath. All Iranians have a split personality."[16]
>
> —Maryam, an Iranian teenager

Traditionally, Iranian families are patriarchal in structure. The father is the head of the household. He is the chief decision maker, primary breadwinner, and spiritual leader of the family. He expects obedience and respect from his wife and children, and he usually gets it. Although approximately 30 percent of Iranian women work outside the home, women are responsible for child rearing and running and maintaining the household. The nation's laws support this structure, giving superior legal status to men. For instance, if a couple divorces, the law automatically grants the father custody of the children.

Children are the center of a married couple's life. Girls are usually more sheltered than boys, especially after they reach puberty. In Iranian culture a daughter is considered a precious jewel. If she is modest and chaste, she can marry well and bring honor to her family. If not, she can ruin her family's standing in society. Therefore, protecting her virtue is vital. Indeed, from a young age boys are taught that they must help protect their family's honor. It is not unusual to see little boys scolding their sisters for any action that shows a lack of modesty.

Both sons and daughters are doted upon by their parents. Wealthy families often buy teenage children expensive jewelry, designer clothes, and luxury cars. Yet Iranian youngsters are rarely spoiled. As soon as they are old enough to understand, they are taught to respect and trust their parents and to put their family's needs above their own.

Children are also raised to be dependent on their parents. Middle-class and wealthy families usually support their children until they finish their education and secure well-paying employment. Poorer families provide whatever financial support they can.

This dependency goes beyond financial support and extends into adulthood. Typically, parents are closely involved in making major decisions in their grown children's lives, including their career choice and spouse selection. Unlike in the West, where a couple's decision to marry is a private matter, in Iran both sets of parents play a vital role in the process. In many cases mothers scout out prospective mates for their children. In other cases the prospective couple already knows and cares for each other. They then share their interest in each other with their mothers. In either situation, once a prospective mate is identified, the mothers arrange one or more get-togethers between the couple and their parents. This allows the young people and the families to interact and get to know each other better. It is important that everyone get along, share common values, and feel they can trust each other, because when individuals marry, their families become entwined. Generally, the new relatives become privy to each other's private home lives. Also, in many cases the families

A family in Tehran makes a snowman. Children are doted upon by their parents and are often the center of attention.

merge business and financial interests. In fact, before a couple weds, their families draw up a marriage contract that specifies a wide array of financial details.

Extended Family

The new in-laws become part of each other's extended families. Extended family members form a complex group, similar to a tribe, that includes grandparents, aunts, uncles, nieces, nephews, and cousins, as well as non-blood relations who are connected to each other via marriage. Such groups can be quite large. Often, extended family members live close together in family compounds or on the same street. But even if they do not, Iranians consider extended family ties to be extremely important. As D.D., an American woman married to an Iranian, explains, "Their lives are like a big spider web. Each life is intricately woven together. . . . As Americans we are individuals doing our own thing. . . . This is not true of Iranian culture."[17]

> "Their lives are like a big spider web. Each life is intricately woven together. . . . As Americans we are individuals doing our own thing. . . . This is not true of Iranian culture."[17]
>
> —D.D., an American woman married to an Iranian man

The large web that extended family forms creates a supportive network that is available when family members need help finding employment, caring for the sick and elderly, assisting with child care, or providing financial support. Grandmothers typically take care of new mothers and babies for at least ten days after the birth. And extended family members have been known to offer their savings or the deed to their homes to help relatives in financial or legal trouble. In fact, it is common for successful family members to help support poorer ones. Moreover, large family groups often share ownership of businesses and property and take out loans as a unit. This is not surprising, since family members trust each other.

Iranian families also come together to celebrate special events and religious festivals. Those who live far apart stay connected via frequent Skyping, as well as journeying to and staying in each other's homes. Therefore, Iranian teens are used to having houseguests. Hospitality is a vital part of Islamic teachings and Iranian

Iranian Weddings

Once a couple becomes engaged, wedding plans begin. Iranians typically have elaborate weddings that are extremely costly. All wedding expenses are paid by the groom's parents. The bride's family is expected to provide the couple with furniture, linens, cookware, appliances, and other large and small items needed to start a new home, as well as a gift of cash, jewelry, and/or property. Among the wealthiest families, the last may even include a house or apartment. This is important because unmarried children usually live with their parents until they wed, so they bring few of their own household items into the marriage. The parents' vital involvement in the wedding itself and in helping set the couple up in their new life tightens both the parents' bond with the couple and their control over them.

In addition, before a couple marries, they and their parents agree on a set amount of money that the groom is required to pay the bride in case they divorce in the future. This is done because a husband has the right to divorce his wife at any time. The husband is not required to pay alimony or provide any financial support to his ex-wife. A wife has no say in the matter and cannot divorce her husband without the husband's permission. In some cases the couple adds a clause to their marriage contract that gives the woman the same divorce rights as the man.

culture. In Iran, according to author Margaret Shaida, "a guest is a gift from God."[18] And because the web of extended family is so complex, it is not unusual for the guests to be virtual strangers who are friends or acquaintances of distant relatives.

A Variety of Homes

Houseguests are welcomed into a variety of homes. The type of home young Iranians grow up in depends on the location and the family's financial status. But no matter the type of building, Iranian homes provide teens a safe place where they can be themselves away from the restrictions of public life.

Teens growing up in cities often live in an apartment building. The apartments of wealthy families are frequently located in luxurious high-rise buildings surrounded by tall, locked gates. Inside the gates are fountains, reflecting pools, and artfully planted greenery. The buildings themselves feature ornate lobbies, banks of elevators, and many of the amenities found in posh hotels. Author Jamie Maslin describes his friend Ali's residence:

> Two huge security gates opened up for us, revealing a palatial, ultramodern apartment building. A beautifully tiled driveway led past several floodlit fountains showering a vast pool, and down to an underground parking area. Inside it was like a five-star hotel with a vast lobby decorated in marble and gold and carpeted with an exquisite Persian rug. In the basement there was a full gym, a communal swimming pool, steam room, and sauna.[19]

Less privileged urban teens live in small one- or two-room houses made of metal and concrete or in comfortable but more modest apartment complexes that are usually shielded by exterior walls that keep out street noise. Rural teens often grow up in small houses that may look unappealing from the outside but are quite comfortable within. Author Nicholas Jubber describes his friend Khamandar's rural home:

> Khamandar and his family lived in a rickety old brick house just off the village's main street, where the railings teetered off the third story balcony like they weren't sure to which floor they belonged. . . . When you ventured outside through the abandoned ground floor, it was like you were wading through a ship that's got itself stuck on the mudflats. But [inside] no household could ever have been as warm.[20]

Other rural teens grow up in sprawling compounds in which multiple family members reside. Each family group has its own set of rooms, but everyone shares a kitchen. Typically, all the rooms open onto a courtyard, where fountains bubble, pomegranate trees blossom, and caged birds sing. Here family members drink tea, relax, and visit as children play and teens hang out together. Still other rural teens live in unique homes that are carved like steps, one above the next, into the sides of mountains. One dwelling's roof serves as the yard of the one above it.

Whether urban or rural, lavish or modest, most Iranian homes have electricity and piped-in water and natural gas. Most have modern stoves, refrigerators, and color television sets. And, although they are illegal, almost every Iranian home has a satellite dish on the balcony or roof. The dishes make it possible for teens and their parents to see banned movies and television shows from Europe and North America. Every so often government officials raid houses and apartment buildings to confiscate the dishes. Residents often know about the raids in advance, though, and hide the dishes. If a dish is confiscated, families can usually pay a fee to unethical officials in exchange for a new dish. As one man explains, "If it's confiscated in an official raid, the technical guys who take it will come back later and install even better gear. But it will cost you."[21]

Inside, Iranian homes are usually decorated with colorful Persian rugs. Most homes have Western-style furniture, as well as big, fluffy cushions along the walls that supply a place to lounge. Most middle- and upper-class Iranian teens have their own bedroom or share a room with a sibling. In poorer families everyone may sleep in a common room that serves as a living room by day and a bedroom at night. Family members sleep on pallets that are rolled up in the day and unrolled at night.

Wealthier young people usually sleep on Western-style beds in bedrooms that resemble those of Western teens. Posters of sports and pop stars decorate the walls, jeans and sneakers fill the closets, and CDs and DVDs line the shelves. Although many of these items are forbidden in Iran, teens do not have to hide them within the haven of their home. Says Jubber of his friend Sina's house:

> "The house was a treasure trove of all that was forbidden in public. . . . If you were a member of the morality police—the basijis—you would be clicking your tongue all the way down the corridor."[22]
>
> —Nicholas Jubber, an author and world traveler

> The house was a treasure trove of all that was forbidden in public. . . . If you were a member of the morality police—the basijis—you would be clicking your tongue all the way down the corridor. You'd be flaring your nostrils at the poster of the bare-headed actress flapping over the desk in Sina's bedroom, as well as several pairs of black market Calvin Kleins, and if you took a few steps down the corridor to Tahmineh's [Sina's sister] room, you would find . . . the pile of banned pre-revolution DVDs under her dressing table.[22]

Food for Everyone

No matter what type of home Iranian youngsters grow up in, when it comes to mealtime, chances are the food will be plentiful and delicious. Iranian cuisine is world famous, as is Iranian hospitality. In the past Iranians ate their meals seated cross-legged around a *sofreh*, a brightly colored cloth embroidered with poetry and prayers that was spread on the floor. Instead of using cutlery, they ate with their fingers. Today most Iranians gather around a dining room table for meals and use a fork and spoon. But most still drape the tabletop with a *sofreh*.

Iranian mealtime features an abundance of delicious foods. This family dines in the traditional manner: seated on the floor around a cloth called a sofreh.

Families Celebrate Norooz

One of the most important holidays in Iran is Norooz (New Day), the Persian New Year. It is one of the few Iranian holidays that is not tied to Islam. Norooz falls on the first day of spring, but the celebration actually goes on for two weeks. It is a time for family gatherings, special family dinners, picnics, and all-out multigenerational fun.

The festival begins with mothers and daughters cleaning the family home. Shopping for new clothes is next. Everyone in the family gets a new outfit for the holiday. Food shopping is also on the agenda; families stock up on pastries, nuts, and dried and fresh fruits to serve to the many friends and family who drop by during the celebratory period.

At sunset on the last Tuesday before Norooz, small bonfires are lit throughout the country. Teenagers celebrate by setting off fireworks and jumping over the fires while chanting a poem about the fire's glow. In a ritual that resembles trick-or-treating, younger children wear costumes and go door to door banging on an empty bowl, which neighbors fill with treats.

On Norooz itself, everyone gathers for a big family dinner. On display are seven items whose names begin with the letter *S*. Each symbolizes an important aspect of life, such as health, happiness, and prosperity.

Finally, on the thirteenth day of the new year (Norooz is the first) families load up baskets with food and go on a picnic. This marks the end of the Norooz celebration.

What is served depends on the time of day and the family. Almost all Iranians follow strict Islamic dietary rules that prohibit the eating of pork and unscaled fish. These laws also forbid the drinking of alcohol and the eating of carnivorous animals and animals that are not slaughtered in a humane manner. Prohibited foods are known as *haram*, whereas permitted foods are known as *halal*.

The woman of the house usually shops for, prepares, and serves the food. Iranian cities and towns have modern supermarkets, bazaars, and small stores where a variety of food is sold. Bakeries abound. Flatbread fresh from the oven is a staple at almost every meal. Hot flatbread served with feta cheese, fresh fruit preserves, yogurt, and tea is a popular breakfast. Families usually eat this meal together. "Sobaneh [*breakfast* in Farsi] is a very important and pleasant moment in the life of an Iranian family," says author Najmieh Batmanglij, "a time to be together before everyone leaves for work."[23] Lunch, which most youngsters eat at school, is typically a light meal that consists of fruit, cheese, nuts, yogurt, and bread.

To tide them over until supper, Iranians have an afternoon snack. On their way home from school, some youngsters stop at fast-food establishments with names like Pizza Hat and Mash Donald's that serve pizza, cheeseburgers, and chicken sandwiches. Other youngsters may stop to buy a hot baked potato from a street vendor.

Dried fruit or pastries accompanied by hot tea or a refreshing cold drink are other afternoon favorites. Iranian pastries are

Iranian women enjoy black tea in a traditional teahouse. Tea is often accompanied by flaky pastries as an afternoon repast.

light and flaky, filled with ground nuts and honey and topped with rose-scented syrup. Hot black tea is served in tiny glasses. Iranians do not add sugar to the glass. Instead, they put a lump of sugar between their teeth and suck the tea through it. The procedure is harder than it sounds. Says Maslin, "It was far from easy, as the whole cube kept falling apart in my mouth so I had to keep getting new cubes. Where I might have had one lump, I now wound up having seven or eight."[24]

Supper is the main meal of the day, and families usually gather together to eat it. What is served varies. But nourishing soups and stews made with bits of lamb, onions, dried limes, beans, and fresh herbs are likely to be on the menu. Kebabs, juicy chunks of lamb threaded on metal skewers and grilled to perfection, are another favorite. Almost every dish is accompanied by hot flatbread and fluffy white rice. Bowls filled with accompaniments such as cucumber slices, tomatoes and onions, and yogurt and spinach dip dot the table for family members to help themselves. Dessert is typically a variety of fresh seasonal fruit.

Families Work and Play Together

Mothers are often assisted by their daughters in preparing and serving meals. Young female family members serve guests and, in many cases, their brothers and father. This helps prepare them for their future role as wives and mothers. After spending the night at the home of two teenage brothers, Maslin was served breakfast. He recalls, "Being the men of the household, the brothers didn't lift a finger at breakfast, which was served for us by their adorable little sisters."[25]

Sisters also help care for their younger siblings. But they are not alone in helping out. Iranian families work together. In rural families, both girls and boys do farm chores, while the sons of artisans, such as rug weavers, start helping their fathers at a young age. In this way they learn the craft.

Moreover, the oldest son in every family is charged with extra responsibilities. If his parents become sick or too old to work, he is expected to take on the responsibilities of the head of the family. This is the case no matter the son's age. Indeed, many male teens and young adults are the sole support of their mothers and siblings.

Iranian family life is not all work and responsibilities, however. Whether it is gathering around the television in the evening to watch their favorite programs, taking family vacations to the Caspian Sea, or picnicking in a local park, Iranian families have fun together. The trust they have in each other makes their homes a refuge from the outside world and makes their relationship very special.

CHAPTER THREE

Education and Work

For thousands of years education and learning have been an important part of Iranian culture. In fact, archaeologists have found twenty-five-hundred-year-old clay tablets covered with markings made by Persian schoolchildren. Today, according to the World Bank, 98.7 percent of Iranians ages fifteen through twenty-four are literate.

Modern Iranians understand that their future financial stability strongly depends on their education level. Although being educated does not guarantee that young Iranians find a well-paying job, it does give candidates an edge in an extremely competitive job market.

Getting an Education

Education is compulsory for Iranian children ages six to fourteen and voluntary for students ages fifteen through eighteen. Children are required to attend five years of primary school and three years of lower secondary school, which translates to grades one through nine. More than 80 percent go on to upper secondary school, which takes three years to complete.

There are about 18 million school-age children in Iran. Most attend public schools, which do not charge tuition. Many public schools, especially those in urban areas, are overcrowded. It is not unheard of for classes to have fifty students. Because of overcrowding, students in public schools do not receive much individualized attention, and teachers do not always have enough time to adequately cover required subject matter. Writer Shervin Malekzadeh explains, "One longtime educator explained to me that for most public-school principals just getting the kids into the building in the morning, then out in the afternoon . . . is what passes for accomplishment."[26] Moreover, like public schools in many countries, Iranian public schools are often in poor physical condition and lack sufficient materials, especially high-tech equipment such as computers. Therefore, many families send their children to private school.

In comparison to public schools, these institutions are less crowded, offer smaller classes and more individualized instruction, and have modern facilities and equipment, including computers and other high-tech learning tools. As a result, private school students have a better chance of doing well on stringent college admission exams than their public school peers. But getting a superior education does not come cheaply. Private schools are expensive. Some parents take on two or three jobs in order to pay the tuition. Many private schools are also difficult to get into. The most prestigious require that students rank high on an admission exam and that transfer students have the equivalent of a 4.0 grade point average.

> "Most teachers are strict and expect great respect and hard work from their students. When the teacher arrives in the classroom, everybody stands up as a sign of respect. They are expected to remain silent in the class until they are called on."[27]
>
> —Malihe Maghazei, an Iranian author and scholar

Courses, Work, and Exams

Iranian schools follow a national curriculum. This means that the course of study is similar for all students whether they attend a public or private school. School calendars are also alike. The school year runs from September through June, Sunday through Thursday. Schools are closed on Friday and Saturday in observance of the Muslim holy day of worship which falls on Friday. The school day usually begins at 7:30 a.m. and ends at 1:00 p.m. In secondary school this schedule translates to four class periods each day, separated by breaks for snacks, rest, and prayer.

Iranian schools are segregated by gender; boys and girls attend separate schools, where they are taught by teachers of the same sex. Students and faculty alike are required to wear uniforms that are in keeping with Islamic law. Head scarves for female students and faculty are common, as are dark slacks and a school shirt for males.

Although the faculty and students may dress alike, classroom dynamics are quite formal. Teachers are accorded a great deal of respect, and students are expected to follow school rules. According to Iranian author and scholar Malihe Maghazei, "Most teachers are strict and expect great respect and hard work from their students. When the teacher arrives in the classroom, everybody stands up as a sign of respect. They are expected to remain silent in the class until they are called on."[27] Misbehavior is not taken lightly, and repeat offenders face expulsion.

The course work, too, is demanding. Students in primary and lower secondary school study math, science, Persian language arts, social studies, study skills, and the Islamic religion. The language of instruction is Farsi, but pupils also learn Arabic as part

Schools in Iran are segregated by gender. Female students wear head scarves as part of their uniform, as do their teachers, who are always of the same gender as the students.

of their study of the Koran, which is written in Arabic. In addition, from first grade onward youngsters are indoctrinated with government propaganda. Textbooks express the government's worldview, encouraging students to adhere to Islamic values and reject Western culture. As one student explains, "In school, we had to learn to pray. . . . We had to chant 'Death to America' every morning, and to pass each grade we had to talk about how much we hated America and how much we loved [the Islamic Prophet] Mohammad."[28]

From first grade on, youngsters are under enormous pressure to do well in school. Their school performance has a huge impact on their future. Students take comprehensive exams twice a year. They must pass these exams in order to move up in grade level and to go from primary to lower secondary school.

Once students complete lower secondary school, if they want to attend upper secondary school, they must successfully complete an admission exam. Their test score combined with their

Military Service

Iran has the eighth-largest military force in the world. Troops are trained in warfare so that they can defend Iran from foreign and internal threats. At age eighteen all young men are required to serve in the military for a period of eighteen to twenty-four months. Those young men who want to serve at a younger age may enlist at age sixteen. Women are forbidden from serving in the military.

About 80 percent to 85 percent of young Iranian males report for military service at age eighteen. Young men who attend college or graduate school can postpone their required military service until they complete their education. Individuals with certain medical conditions are exempt from service. Only-sons whose fathers are dead or whose fathers are over age seventy are exempt too, since typically these young men serve as the head of their families. Individuals studying to be clerics are also exempt from military service. Some wealthy young men pay high fees to buy off their required service, which gains them an exemption. Those young men who do not have an exemption and do not serve in the military face a difficult future. They are ineligible for government jobs and are often not hired for high-paying jobs in other sectors. In addition, they are not allowed to apply for a passport.

grade point average determines whether they qualify for upper secondary school, the specific school they may attend, and the focus of their studies. Those with the best numbers gain seats in academic schools that focus on preparing students for college. Lower scorers are placed in technical schools that prepare them for lower-level technical and applied science careers. Those who do not make either cut have the option of receiving vocational training in a specific trade or entering the workforce.

Students in small rural villages face more constraints than their urban counterparts. There are few upper secondary schools in rural areas, so teens may have to commute to larger towns to continue their education. This is particularly problematic for girls, who are often quite sheltered by their parents. Asma is one of these girls. Although she wanted to continue her education, her family did not permit it. Her mother, Bari Khatoum, explains, "If the secondary school was in the village, I wouldn't have minded so much. But because there is no school nearby, Asma would have had to catch a bus and that is not good."[29]

All upper secondary students study a common curriculum for the first two years, which includes Islamic studies, English as a foreign language, Arabic, Persian literature, various sciences, mathematics, and Iranian history and geography. In the third year, students focus on a specific area of concentration that prepares them for a college major in this field and/or their future career. What this area may be is determined by students' ranking on their admission exam, their grade point average, and, to a lesser extent, their personal preference. Students in technical schools focus on one of three fields: agriculture, technology, or business. Students in academic schools focus on math and physics, experimental sciences, religion, or humanities and literature. A concentration in math and physics requires the highest ranking. Students must work extra hard to qualify for this specialty.

No matter the area of specialization, homework is a major part of education in Iran. From first grade onward, students are given lots of homework. Many parents assist youngsters with their homework, and some hire private homework tutors. Indeed, the pressure to succeed is so intense that many children and teens work on supplemental educational material when their homework is complete. Some attend private classes in the evenings and during school vacations to sharpen their academic skills. As an

Iranian mother explains, "I'd like to see my child doing extra practice on what she has learned at school. There are plenty of published supplementary books out there in the market . . . and I feel stressed if I don't get them for my child. She needs to work hard to get to a good school and be successful in the future."[30]

University Admissions

Families that can afford the cost also hire tutors, purchase educational supplementary materials, and enroll teens in special classes to help them prepare for the Konkur, an extremely rigorous college admissions exam. Young people usually start preparing for the test at least a year in advance. In the months before the test, many youngsters and their families go into what is known as "Konkur quarantine." They avoid social events and family gatherings so that teens are not distracted from their studies.

> "I'd like to see my child doing extra practice on what she has learned at school. . . . She needs to work hard to get to a good school and be successful in the future."[30]
>
> —The mother of an Iranian primary school student

The pressure to do well on the test is intense. A lot rides on a youngster's performance. Students are admitted to free public universities based on their test scores, and private colleges use student test results, in addition to other criteria, in determining admission. Admittance standards vary depending on a student's field of study. The number of open slots in each field differs. Competition for a place in a field like engineering, a very popular and prestigious field of study in Iran, is intense and requires a higher ranking than for a less popular field like literature. Moreover, in the past decade, many Iranian colleges have taken to limiting or completely banning female students' access to approximately seventy fields of study. No official reason has been offered for this action. Teen Leila explains, "I wanted to study architecture and civil engineering. But access for girls has been cut by fifty per cent, and there's a chance I won't get into university at all this year."[31]

More than 1 million individuals take the Konkur each year. In 2016 only 10 percent were admitted to public universities. Students with low or failing scores can take the test again the follow-

A professor conducts a class at Tehran University. College admission standards vary according to the field of study, and there are often only a certain number of slots that can be filled for each area.

ing year; some take the exam several times before gaining college admission. It is not uncommon for young people who fail the test to become depressed.

Although college admissions and a student's major are largely determined by the Konkur, some young people are given preference over their peers because of their loyalty and devotion to the government or due to their connection to important people. These students include members of the Basij, as well as those with family connections to high-ranking clerics or other government officials. According to Saeid Golkar, author and visiting fellow for Iran policy at the Chicago Council on Global Affairs, about 40 percent of public college slots are reserved for Basijis.

Higher Education

Of those young people admitted to college, 49 percent attend public universities. Despite restrictions, more than 60 percent of all college entrants in Iran are women. Although Iranian colleges are coed, male-female interaction is discouraged. Students are expected to self-segregate in cafeterias, libraries, lecture halls,

Young Iranians and Drug Addiction

Frustration with their inability to find suitable employment leads some Iranian teens to turn to drug abuse. The United Nations Office on Drugs and Crime estimates that 2.2 percent of Iran's population are drug addicts, making Iran the nation with the highest drug addiction rate in the world. Many experts put the real figure as even higher.

Many of these addicts are teens and young adults. Opium is the most popular drug, and it is easy to obtain. Iran's neighbor Afghanistan is the world's leading source of the drug. Tons of opium are smuggled from Afghanistan through Iran and on to Europe each year.

The Iranian government spends a lot of money fighting a war on drugs. Troops are posted at the borders, and individuals found guilty of smuggling drugs are executed. The government also provides methadone clinics to help addicts kick their habit, as well as needle exchanges to prevent addicts from sharing needles, an activity that can spread blood-borne diseases like hepatitis.

and other common areas. Some universities have gender-specific entrance and exit gates as well as partitions in common areas to accommodate segregation. To discourage inappropriate activities, student Basijis monitor the dress and behavior of their peers. Couples caught walking together, holding hands, or simply hanging out face reprimands. According to one college student, "They [Basijis] . . . wait for any motivation against their interests so that they can scream and yell."[32]

The entry gates to Iranian colleges are guarded by armed security personnel. Otherwise—with the exception of designated prayer areas, on-campus mosques, and large posters of the supreme leader hanging from many buildings—the campuses do not look very different from those in North America. Author Jared Cohen describes what he saw on a visit to the University of Tehran:

Students sat in scattered circular formations throughout the grass courtyards. . . . Other students crowded onto the stairs of the building, perfectly situated for optimal people watching. . . . I turned to enter the first building I saw. It was a three-story cement structure decorated with elaborate columns in front. . . . Inside, students were running wild, dashing in different directions and forming pockets of loud, chattering social groups in every square inch of the lobby. Others ran to the cafeteria to get a sandwich or a muffin before their next class. There were even some who I saw taking a nap on the floor. It reminded me of the period in between classes in an American high school, where students make use of those few minutes of liberation from the classroom.[33]

When possible, college students live at home with their families. If this is not feasible, they live in single-gender college dormitories. Usually four students are crowded into a small dorm room.

When students are not studying, they can participate in clubs, academic contests, and athletic activities. Some students become political activists. These young people demonstrate and speak out against the government. However, such activities come with a steep price. Known activists are graded on a special politically motivated star system whose purpose is to expel them from college, no matter their academic performance. Still, many feel so strongly that they persist in these activities despite the threat of dismissal.

Getting a Job

Finding a good, well-paying job in Iran is challenging. About 1 million young Iranians enter the job market each year. This number far exceeds the number of available positions. As of 2016 unemployment among Iranians ages fifteen through twenty-four was 26 percent, more than twice the general unemployment rate. Although having a college degree increases an individual's chances of getting a good job, it does not guarantee it. In fact, on average, it takes college graduates up to three years to obtain suitable employment.

Many graduates depend on family connections to get a job. Nepotism, a practice in which favoritism is given to family and friends when filling a position, is an accepted part of Iranian culture. Although this practice helps many individuals, it puts those without such connections at a distinct disadvantage.

Young women, too, are at a disadvantage. They often have unequal access to many jobs. The jobless rate for women is about one and a half times that of men. As British journalist David Blair reports, "Over the summer, the Iranian Central Bank advertised various positions intended for university graduates. . . . Of the 47 vacancies, 36 were 'men only' and 11 were available to both genders. The logic behind the distinction was unclear. For some reason, men and women can join the 'statistics' section of the Central Bank—but the 'accounting' department is men only."[34]

Moreover, getting a position does not guarantee financial independence. Salaries, even for highly educated men and women, are low. Numbeo, a database of living conditions throughout the world, reports that as of 2017 the average monthly salary in

A technician works on a car in an auto factory. Finding a well-paying job is challenging in Iran, where the number of people seeking employment exceeds the number of available positions, and having a college degree does not guarantee employment.

Tehran was the equivalent of $513 (US dollars). In comparison, the website estimates that monthly expenses for a single person (not including rent) were equal to $461 (US dollars). Fatema, a young blogger, explains:

> I was so lucky that [I] could get this job as an engineer, in a rather good, big company in Tehran. . . . I love it to be financially independent, however, it's not easy to call it "independent." If I do some simple calculations like this: I should save all my salary for 3 years continuously to afford a car, I should save it all for 13 years to be able to buy the smallest cheapest apartment in the worst location of Tehran, I should pay all my monthly salary to rent that apartment! But it's still OK, I keep living with my family. . . . Most other Iranians are living the same situation.[35]

Many young, educated Iranians become so discouraged with the lack of opportunity that they seek employment in other countries. According to the International Monetary Fund, more than 150,000 college-educated Iranians leave the country every year, giving Iran one of the world's highest rates of "brain drain." As Kimia, a young woman hoping to move to Germany, explains, "A person wants to stay in their own country. . . . But I tell myself that maybe there I'll be successful, and my children will benefit from that success. Not here. I have no future here."[36]

Young people with limited education have even less opportunity. Some learn ancient trades like rug weaving from members of their families. Others work on family farms. Many head for Iranian cities in search of employment. However, there are few jobs for unskilled laborers. Some youngsters find low-paying work in stores, restaurants, and garages. Those with cars often provide a type of taxi service in which they give rides to passengers for a set fee. Others, many of them

"Over the summer, the Iranian Central Bank advertised various positions intended for university graduates. . . . Of the 47 vacancies, 36 were 'men only' and 11 were available to both genders. The logic behind the distinction was unclear."[34]

—David Blair, a British journalist

children, become street vendors. Still others turn to black market activities, selling contraband items such as banned DVDs, CDs, and liquor to wealthy Iranians. However, if they are caught, they face fines and/or imprisonment.

It is clear that when it comes to education and work, Iranian teens face many challenges. Students must work very hard in school in order to continue their education. In addition to their schoolwork, many youngsters work on supplemental materials in their free time in an effort to get ahead. However, even top scholars are not guaranteed a well-paying job. Iranians ages fifteen through twenty-four face high unemployment. As one discouraged college student explains, "We are proud people and there is no opportunity for us. Sometimes we question what will be our future."[37]

CHAPTER FOUR

Social Life

Iranian teenagers are like young people everywhere. They like to have fun. Hanging out with friends, listening to music, using social media, participating in and watching sporting events, and going to parties are just a few of the activities they enjoy. However, many of these activities are prohibited in Iran because religious leaders believe they undermine Islamic values.

Some Iranian teens are extremely devout; they find fulfillment through their religion. Others think that laws restricting how and with whom they socialize are too strict. Although Iranians face punishment if they are caught participating in banned activities, many teens find ways to circumvent laws they do not like. As Nazanin, a young woman, explains, "When foreigners look at TV they don't see the real Iran. We have the surface society and we have the underground society. We have our parties, we get drunk, nothing is legal. We live like in the west . . . but we still have to worry about the police, they can catch you for anything. Of course you can get around them, especially if you have money and you can pay bribes."[38]

Trusted Friends

Spending time with friends is an important part of teen life in Iran. Iranian teens do not take friendship lightly. In a nation where a slip of the tongue can get individuals into serious trouble and the authorities encourage youngsters to disclose damaging information about their peers, Iranian teens are careful in whom they confide. Friends must be able to trust each other in the same way that they trust their families. As Iranian British author Ramita Navai explains, "In such an oppressive environment, everything is heightened. Friendships mean that much more; relationships are that much stronger. Trust is everything when you can get in trouble so easily. So you have to be careful whom you let close, and whom you trust."[39]

Friendships are almost always between young people of the same gender. Considering Iranian culture and laws, this is not surprising. What may be surprising is how affectionate same-sex friends are with each other. Friends usually greet each other with a hug or a kiss on the cheek. They often walk arm in arm or hold hands. Such displays are not sexual in nature, but rather a way friends show fondness for each other. As author Nicholas Jubber recalls, "Sina [Jubber's friend] would innocently take my hand when he was leading me over the road and kisses of men's cheeks were a common ritual on the threshold of the house."[40]

> "In such an oppressive environment, everything is heightened. . . . Trust is everything when you can get in trouble so easily. So you have to be careful whom you let close, and whom you trust."[39]
>
> —Ramita Navai, an award-winning Iranian British journalist

Friends do lots of things together. They usually meet and/or communicate regularly. They chat and laugh, go to movies and concerts, and visit museums and art galleries. They shop, play sports, take day trips to the mountains, and study together. "We like and we do everything like other youth around the world,"[41] Mariam, an Iranian teen, explains.

Dating

In Iran social relationships between unmarried men and women who are not related are forbidden. Law enforcement personnel patrol cities and towns looking for lawbreakers. Unmarried couples who are caught walking or sitting close together, holding hands, dancing, or embracing, among other activities, face punishment. Hamid, a young Iranian man, recalls his experience: "I was walking with my girlfriend in the street and the police took us. I was in prison for a day and I got beaten twenty lashes with a whip. The police were very angry."[42]

Yet despite the risk, Iranian teens still manage to spend time together. Unlike in most Western nations, where boys and girls interact daily, in Iran males and females are largely segregated.

This makes it difficult for young people to meet members of the opposite sex. Flirting with or chatting up an attractive stranger is risky. Instead, when young adults see a person whom they are interested in meeting, they stealthily pass a small piece of paper with their contact information to that individual. These notes are passed in libraries, shopping malls, parks, and cafés; on college campuses; and between cars caught in traffic jams. Author Jamie Maslin met an Iranian girl in this manner. He recalls, "Without my asking, she wrote down her e-mail address for me, seconds before her mother joined us. . . . The girl gestured to the piece of paper with her e-mail and said, 'Secret cannot tell.'"[43]

Since informal dating is forbidden, when boys and girls do get together for such a purpose, they do so in a private setting. Many keep their relationship secret from their parents, who may disapprove of the connection or worry about the possible consequences. Some couples meet in secluded areas away from

Young people in Iran value friendship and choose their friends carefully. Trust is an especially important factor among friends in Iran.

prying eyes. A popular way for couples to socialize is at private underground parties, which are held in homes, apartments, and abandoned buildings. In some cases liberal parents who want their teenage children to develop healthy relationships allow teens to throw the party. But in most incidences, teens plan and attend these gatherings without their parents' knowledge.

> "We want more freedom. We want places to listen to music, socialize, meet people—like in the U.S."[46]
>
> —Mohammad, an Iranian college student

What goes on at these parties depends on the host. Some parties are relatively tame—boys and girls wear Western-style fashions, chat and flirt, dance to forbidden music, and enjoy snack foods. Other parties are more like Western-style raves, featuring illegal drinking, drug abuse, and promiscuity. As an Iranian student living in Europe jokes, "There is more vodka than in Russia."[44]

It is not uncommon for underground parties to be raided by the police. Sometimes officials let the lawbreakers go in exchange for a monetary bribe. In other cases they arrest and even rough up the guests. Author Ali Delforoush describes such a raid:

> Military SUVs smashed through the gates and entered the complex, while officers armed with batons rushed out towards the entrance of the complex. . . . Women in short dresses and skirts began to desperately cover their exposed skin and hair, while the men frantically placed stacks of chewing gum in their mouths in attempts to mask the smell of alcohol. . . . Omid [the author's friend] . . . saw a number of uniforms making their way up the stairs, arresting and hauling boys and girls out of the complex.[45]

Despite the risk, underground parties are common. In addition to providing an opportunity to socialize with the opposite sex, these parties allow young people, forced to live under rigid laws, to let off steam and exercise their personal freedom. As Mohammad, a college student, explains, "We want more freedom. We want places to listen to music, socialize, meet people—like in the U.S."[46]

Internet Dating

Dating websites like Match.com and eHarmony are banned in Iran. Iranian software engineers, however, have developed local dating websites much like American ones. The websites, which present profiles and display photos of singles looking for a relationship, charge membership fees. Since dating is prohibited in Iran, these websites are illegal, so many of them are marketed as marriage websites rather than dating websites to avoid being shut down by the government.

The Iranian government has responded by introducing its own state-sponsored spouse-finding website. Visitors to the site answer a personal questionnaire and are then matched to compatible mates. Online "counselors" monitor users to ensure that Islamic values are maintained and rules concerning social relationships are followed. The website was established in June 2015. According to the Iranian government, in the following seven months sixteen thousand Iranians registered on the site, leading to 140 marriages.

Staying Connected

One way teens spread the word about underground parties is via the Internet. E-mail, instant messaging, texting, online forums, and social media provide young Iranians an important way to connect with each other and with the outside world. Iranian teens use the Internet to meet and flirt with members of the opposite sex, organize demonstrations and underground social events, get news from other countries, and give outsiders a better understanding of what life is like in Iran. As journalist Roula Khalaf explains, "The boys and girls of the Islamic Republic . . . spend their lives on social media—Viber [an instant messaging and voice-over app] is the latest craze, and a forum for jokes about their leaders."[47]

The *CIA World Factbook* reports that as of July 2015, 44.1 percent of Iranians had access to the Internet, and according to Iran's Ministry of Communications, as of 2015, 20 million Iranians had smartphones. Many national and international news sites are banned in Iran. So are American social media websites such as Twitter, Facebook, and YouTube, among others. Visiting or posting on these sites is forbidden by the government. But it is difficult to enforce these bans. Even though the government maintains cyberpolice whose job is to monitor, regulate, and control cyber-space, tech-savvy teens use special software—and/or find indirect methods such as virtual private networks, which are connected to foreign servers—to access banned websites and get around gov-ernment surveillance. Moreover, because the Internet is so vast, it is impossible for the government to effectively monitor everything young people say and do on it. The government has, however, managed to remove some websites, filter the content of others, and slow down connectivity in general. As Holly Dagres, an Iranian American journalist, explains, "Imagine every time you type a URL in your address bar, you're hit by what President Obama called an 'Electronic Curtain,' referring you to a list of sites that are 'mor-ally' approved by the Iranian regime complete with a photo of the Quran [Koran] . . . in the background."[48] In fact, Reporters Without Borders, an international organization that promotes freedom of the press, ranks Iran among the top ten enemies of the Internet.

Despite the bans and slowdowns, the US Department of State estimates that 17 million Iranians have Facebook accounts. Most of these individuals are teens and young adults. Iranian teens also use domestic social media sites run in accordance with Islamic law to communicate. These Iran-based websites feature chat rooms, local news, instant messaging, shopping venues, and blogs.

An estimated seventy-five thousand Iranians are bloggers; most are under thirty years old. Monitoring these blogs is a primary focus of the cyberpolice, who shut down blogs and harass blog-gers who express views contrary to Islamic values. Banned blogs are replaced with an announcement saying, "According to the rules of the Islamic Republic of Iran, access to this site is forbidden."[49] To keep from being identified, many bloggers use assumed names and post from Internet cafés. The latter keeps officials from tracing the computer's Internet protocol address back to the blogger.

Not all Iranian bloggers write about controversial issues. In a nation in which many forms of personal freedom are regu-lated, blogging gives young Iranians a relatively safe forum for self-expression. Iranian blogs deal with anything and everything, ranging from topics like fashion and sports to cooking and po-etry. Indeed, when asked why blogging is so popular in Iran, Ali, an engineering student, explained, "You can tell about anything you want!"[50]

Outdoor Fun

Iranians enjoy the outdoors. The nation has many parks and walking trails where young people gather to talk, picnic, bicycle, and in-line skate. In an effort to enforce sharia law, officials patrol many, but not all, of these areas. Anyone caught violating the law may be arrested. One area where youngsters can escape observation and have fun is the mountains. Iran is home to a number of ski areas and secluded mountain areas where law enforcement is lax. With few individuals monitoring their behavior, teens can ski, snowboard, hike, and climb in relative freedom. Although ski lifts are segregated, once teens get on ski runs it is not unusual for boys and girls to ski or snowboard down together. The slopes also serve as a type of fashion runway for young women, many of whom discard their chadors and scarves for uncovered hair, designer sunglasses, and the latest in ski apparel. As one young female skier explains, "This government tries to configure its people.

With so many nearby mountains, skiing is a popular pastime in Iran. It also allows people more freedom than when they are in the cities, where authorities are always watching.

But the young generation do what they want. . . . It's really nice not to wear the headscarf while skiing. . . . If I had the choice I would never wear it."[51]

Secluded mountain areas also provide young people with places to hike and climb without being watched. Many teens head for the mountains, which are less than a two-hour drive from Tehran, on weekends and holidays. They spend the day climbing upward, stopping to play in the snow, admire the spectacular views, or snack on kebabs cooked in restaurants located along the trail.

For times when it is impossible to get away, many young Iranians practice parkour on Iran's streets and parks. Parkour is a sport based on military obstacle course training. It involves overcoming physical barriers in a new way to get from one point to another. For example, rather than walking around a park bench, parkour practitioners might vault over it. Enthusiasts employ gymnastics, acrobatics, and martial arts–type moves. They climb walls, leap over fences, balance on narrow ledges, run through city streets, jump from rooftop to rooftop, and do backflips off bridges, among other high-flying movements.

The sport is very popular among both boys and girls. Amazingly, the girls perform the daring moves while wearing restrictive garments. It is not surprising that an activity that involves overcoming obstacles and viewing the world in a new way is popular with young Iranians, who are experts at overcoming government-imposed restrictions on a daily basis. As Drew Obenreder, an American parkour athlete, explains, "If you can conquer anything physically, you can do the same thing mentally. And the other way: If you can overcome it mentally, you can overcome it physically."[52]

Moreover, practitioners say that doing parkour makes them feel liberated. Fatemeh Akrami is one of Iran's best-known parkour practitioners. She explains, "The main feeling I get from parkour is freedom. It really helped me to feel that freedom in my own country."[53]

Popular Team Sports

Iranian teens also enjoy participating in and watching a number of team sports. Soccer, or football as it is known in Iran, is probably the most popular. Iranian boys can be seen playing the sport in streets, alleys, parks, soccer fields, and schoolyards everywhere.

Popular Plastic Surgery

Despite the government's emphasis on religion and spiritual values, many young women in Iran are very concerned with outer beauty, especially when it comes to their faces. Approximately two hundred thousand Iranians a year, mostly young women, undergo a type of cosmetic surgery called rhinoplasty to change the shape of their nose.

Iran has the highest rate of nose surgery in the world. In fact, the Rhinology Research Society in Iran conducted a study in conjunction with Johns Hopkins University in the United States comparing the frequency of rhinoplasty surgery in the two nations. The study found that the rate of the surgery is seven times greater in Iran than in the United States.

The surgery involves a surgeon breaking the patient's nose, then reshaping it. It is performed on girls as young as fourteen. Generally, those who undergo the surgery want the size of their noses reduced and the tip made to point upward.

There is no exact reason why the surgery is so popular. An online news article suggests that the surgery is a reaction to the restrictive dress rules placed on women. "They won't let us display our beauty," a woman explains. "It's human nature to want to seek out attention with a beautiful figure, hair, skin, but hijab doesn't let you do that. So we have to satisfy that instinct by displaying our 'art' on our faces."

Quoted in Tehran Bureau Correspondent, "The Beauty Obsession Feeding Iran's Voracious Cosmetic Surgery Industry," *Guardian* (Manchester), March 1, 2013. www.theguardian.com.

Girls wearing head scarves and uniforms that completely cover their arms and legs play in special indoor facilities dedicated to female soccer.

Youngsters not only play soccer, they spend many hours watching soccer matches. Iran is home to both a men's and women's national team that represent Iran in international competitions, as well as many local teams that compete against each other. Gathering around television sets to watch matches is a common social activity for groups of friends and family members no matter their politics or level of religious devotion. Mina, a soccer fan, explains, "No matter the time of day, we're always watching live matches. . . . It's our hobby. . . . My mother—my whole family, really—is religious, and they love . . . football [soccer]. And it's not just me and my family."[54]

Every Iranian city has soccer fields and stadiums. Tehran's Azadi Stadium is the twenty-third-largest soccer stadium in the world, with a capacity of more than seventy-eight thousand spectators. Females are barred from attending male matches in person. Similarly, males are banned from attending women's matches. According to Iranian clerics, mixed crowds watching matches together is contrary to Islamic values. Still, when an Iranian team qualifies for the World Cup or other international event, sexual segregation is forgotten as both males and females take to the streets by the thousands in wild celebration.

Music

Iranian youngsters listen to all kinds of music. As with many other things in Iranian society, some forms of music are forbidden. Such music includes contemporary American and European music, as

A group of female musicians make so-called underground music—music that is forbidden by strict Iranian authorities.

well as local music similar to Western music. To keep youngsters from listening to unapproved music, the government censors local radio stations, allowing them to broadcast only approved music such as traditional Persian folk songs and some classical pieces.

This does not stop Iranian teens. Many youngsters buy bootleg CDs of banned music from black market sellers. And they download or stream music from the Internet. In fact, because it is illegal for Iranian musicians to perform in public without government approval, many Iranian musicians perform online for thousands of teen followers.

Youngsters also organize underground concerts in secluded areas. As with private parties, these concerts are often raided by disciplinary forces. Participants may be arrested and musical instruments confiscated. However, the risk has not lessened the popularity of such events. Ali, a young musician, was arrested twice for playing rock music at underground concerts. He spent twenty days in jail and received ninety lashes as punishment. Yet he refuses to stop. "We're still gonna party, play rock, rap, and do what we want, and if they want to make me stop, then they better cut off both my arms so I can't pick up my guitar again!"[55] he vows.

Rap-e Farsi, rap music performed in Farsi, is especially popular with Iranian teens. Farsi is a poetic language. Traditionally, poetry has always been an important part of Iranian culture. For Iranian rap fans, rap lyrics serve as a modern form of this tradition. The music, however, is controversial. Song lyrics often criticize or mock the government, detail the challenges of daily life in Iran, and encourage social change. Rappers and rap concertgoers are frequently arrested. However, as with many activities that are discouraged or forbidden in Iran, Iranian teens find ways to listen to rap music and take part in activities they enjoy. When it comes to having fun, teens in Iran are no different from their peers all over the world.

CHAPTER FIVE

Religious Influences

Iran is a theocratic republic in which Shia Islam is the official religion. About 99 percent of Iranians are Muslims, and the nation's most powerful official, the supreme leader, is a Muslim cleric. All of the nation's laws are based on the supreme leader and other high-ranking clerics' interpretation of the Koran. Consequently, Islamic culture, traditions, and religious doctrine affect almost every aspect of all young Iranians' lives. For example, schools require that everyone study religion, and prayer is an established part of daily life. The wail of muezzins, or criers, summoning people to prayer five times a day through loudspeakers mounted on mosques is a common sound. And schools and workplaces have dedicated areas where workers and students are expected to pray when the call is heard. Moreover, the state requires that people observe the Sabbath and fast during Ramadan. It also urges all males to attend Friday Sabbath services.

Many young Iranians disagree with the government's rigid interpretation of Islam. They feel that the Koran is meant to be interpreted in an evolutionary manner and that they should be permitted to practice their religion based on their own personal interpretation rather than the government's. As a university professor explains, "Most Iranians are spiritual, but does this oblige us to attend the mosque every Friday and perform the fast in Ramadan? Of course not! These things are external rituals, they are not what matters."[56]

Indeed, the government's involvement in religion has turned some young Iranians away from religious practices. They complain that religion has become too entwined with politics. For example, throughout the nation, two sermons are given during Friday prayer services. One deals with morality and religion, while the other focuses on political issues and state policies. This part includes worshippers chanting anti-Western propaganda. According to Hammid Reza Ahmadabadi, a man who regularly attends Friday services, "We shout death to America, but first we say Allah is great three times, then we shout death to Israel and we end with death to England."[57]

As a consequence, many Iranian teens remain believers of Islam but not practitioners. For example, although many youngsters attend Friday services out of faithfulness to their religion, others refuse. According to author Jared Cohen, "People in Iran view the Friday prayers as having lost its religious essence. Instead, they see it as a forum for the regime to galvanize its few supporters and reaffirm its ideology."[58]

> "We shout death to America, but first we say Allah is great three times, then we shout death to Israel and we end with death to England."[57]
>
> —Hammid Reza Ahmadabadi, an Iranian man who regularly attends Friday services

Religion and Sexuality

Although the Koran prohibits sex before and outside of marriage, many young Iranians disregard Islamic doctrine on this issue. However, since Iran operates under sharia law, breaking this prohibition is dangerous. Girls are considered adults in Iran at age nine; boys are considered adults at age fifteen. From those ages on, girls and boys who are caught having sexual relations face punishment that ranges from imprisonment to execution, depending on the particular incident.

Nevertheless, many young Iranians are sexually active. A large number of these believe they have the right to do what they please with their own bodies without the government dictating Islamic morality. Some see their actions as a way to exert their personal freedom. Others view it as a covert form of protest. As Zahra, a young Iranian woman, says, "Nobody can tell me what I can do with my own body—nobody can tell me how to love."[59]

Considering the consequences of discovery, most sexually active couples keep their relationship secret. This is especially true for young women. Female virginity is highly valued in Iranian

Separated by gender, people participate in the Muslim holiday prayer that concludes the holy month of Ramadan. Religion permeates public and private life in Iran.

culture. According to British Iranian journalist Ramita Navai, it "is seen as a marker of decency, of good family stock and morals. . . . Here, a woman's virtue is the cornerstone of life."[60] The law also requires young men to abstain from sexual relations outside of marriage. However, since it is difficult to prove or disprove whether a male is a virgin, it is easier for young men to keep their sex lives secret.

Indeed, if a young woman is known to be promiscuous, she brings shame to herself and her family. In fact, a woman's virginity is often a condition of marriage in Iran. Grooms-to-be can require that the bride present a certificate of virginity signed by a doctor. Moreover, if a bride falsely claims to be a virgin, the groom can have the marriage annulled. As Bahram, a PhD student in Tehran, explains, "I know many educated men who claim that virginity is not that important to them, but they still won't marry their girl-friends, preferring to have them only as their partners."[61]

Because female virginity is so valued, some nonvirgins undergo a hymenoplasty to conceal their sexual past. This is a surgical procedure in which the membrane that is torn when a woman loses her virginity is reconstructed. Although the surgery is not officially sanctioned under sharia law, it is not forbidden, either. As a matter of fact, Iranian cleric Ayatollah Sadeq Rouhani issued a legal decree that says, "There is no difference between a real and fake hymen."[62] The decree makes it legal for women who undergo the surgery to be certified as virgins.

Other young women do whatever it takes to preserve their virginity. For many, this is more about keeping up appearances than following religious dictates. These women have sexual relations that do not involve their genitals. As Tamineh, a young Iranian woman, explains, "I first had anal sex when I was 21. Of course I want to have proper sex, but until I know for sure that my boyfriend wants to get married, I can't risk it."[63]

> "Nobody can tell me what I can do with my own body—nobody can tell me how to love."[59]
>
> —Zahra, a young Iranian woman

Temporary Marriage

One way young Iranians can have sexual intercourse without breaking Islamic law is by a process known as *sigheh*, or temporary marriage. Sigheh allows couples to meet their physical needs without shaming their family, risking punishment, or going against their religion.

Temporarily married couples draw up a legally binding marriage contract that specifies the terms of the marriage just like permanently married couples. The couple file the contract with a cleric and in turn receive a legal marriage certificate that serves as proof of their marriage. However, unlike in traditional Iranian marriage contracts, which can be terminated only by death or

Islam prohibits sex outside of marriage. Many Iranian teens ignore the prohibition and try to keep their relationships secret, risking imprisonment and even a death penalty in some circumstances.

divorce, temporary marriage contracts contain a specific expiration date ranging from one hour to ninety-nine years, depending on the couple's wishes. Moreover, the contract usually requires that the man pay a predetermined sum known as a *mehr*, which is considered a gift, to his short-term wife.

The man, but not the woman, can break the contract at any time without retribution. When the contract expires, it can be renewed as often as the man desires. Each time it is renewed, another mehr is paid. Children born of sighehs are considered legitimate and entitled to a share of their father's inheritance upon his death. Temporary wives, on the other hand, have no right to inheritance.

Under sharia law, during the terms of the contract, the couple are treated the same as a traditionally wedded couple. Therefore, the couple can interact with each other in public. As Maryam, a young woman who was temporarily married to a man named Karim, explains, "We went out a lot together, and I didn't want to get into trouble. We wanted to have documents so that if we were stopped on the street we could prove we weren't doing anything illegal."[64]

Even though sigheh is acceptable under sharia law, it is controversial. Some Iranians say that the practice is a form of government-endorsed prostitution, especially if a marriage lasts only a few hours. Despite this concern, some young Iranians find temporary marriage to be a positive way for them to both follow religious laws and satisfy their physical desires.

Contraceptives and Abortion

Although sigheh is popular with some Iranians, because the marriage is temporary, many of these couples prefer not to have children together. Proper use of birth control helps them avoid an unwanted pregnancy. It also helps permanently married couples control the size and spacing of their families, and it helps keep sexually active singles from having a baby out of wedlock.

In Iran women who become pregnant outside of wedlock may be sentenced to up to one hundred lashes. Their families often turn them out, and they are shunned by society. If they give birth, their child faces a difficult future. Children born outside of wedlock are not issued a birth certificate and have no rights or protection under the law. A pregnant, unwed university student explains, "I couldn't talk about it with my parents or close friends, and I even considered suicide. I cursed this country where they force Islamic law on us."[65]

The Koran encourages procreation, but it does not make any explicit statements about the morality or immorality of birth control. Therefore, Muslim scholars have differing interpretations about how Islam views the use of contraceptives. These views have changed recently in Iran.

In the 1980s Iran's supreme leader, Ayatollah Ruhollah Khomeini, issued a decree encouraging married couples to practice birth control. The decree was part of a government effort to control population growth. To make it easy for couples to obey the decree, the government set up family planning clinics all over the country that provided free contraceptive devices and legalized sterilization procedures to married couples. Although the clinics did not serve single people, contraceptive devices were readily available on the black market to anyone who wanted them. As a result, population growth was controlled.

Things changed in 2012. That year, in an effort to increase Iran's global power by increasing its population, Ayatollah Ali Khamenei issued a decree condemning family planning. Since then access to contraceptives has become extremely limited, leading to a rise in unwanted pregnancies.

In an effort to end an unwanted pregnancy, some young women seek abortions. As with contraception, there is disagreement among Islamic scholars about whether the Koran permits abortion. In Iran abortion is forbidden unless the health of the mother or fetus is at risk. Iran's Ministry of Health reports that about six thousand legal abortions are performed annually on women who meet these guidelines.

In contrast, according to Dr. Mohammad Esmaeel Motlagh, the director of Iran's Health and Population Bureau, an estimated 250,000 illegal abortions are performed annually in the country. Women who have an illegal abortion face five years in prison and a large fine if they are caught. Still, many desperate women do whatever it takes to terminate an unwanted pregnancy. Some ingest dangerous drugs in an attempt to induce a miscarriage, or they seek expensive clandestine abortions. Many of these procedures are performed by untrained individuals in an unsterile environment. It is not uncommon for botched illegal abortions to cause permanent damage to the woman's reproductive system or her internal organs. Moreover, even if the results threaten a woman's health, medical personnel are required to report her to the authorities if she seeks care at a hospital.

Homosexuality

Homosexual teens face other challenges under sharia law, which forbids same-sex relations. If they are found out, homosexuals receive harsh punishment that includes long-term imprisonment, hundreds of lashes, or even execution. In order to protect themselves, most young gays and lesbians keep their sexual orienta-

Being a Non-Muslim in the Islamic Republic of Iran

One percent of Iran's population is non-Muslim; many are teenagers. Even though these young people do not practice Islam, since they live in a theocracy, they are bound by sharia law just like their Muslim peers. For example, they, too, are prohibited from eating in public during Ramadan, and they must follow state-mandated dress codes and other regulations that affect their personal freedom. If they do not, they face the same penalties as the rest of the population.

Iran's constitution recognizes and guarantees freedom of religion for Christians, Jews, and Zoroastrians, adherents of a religion that began in ancient Persia. The government protects the followers of these religions and allows them to openly practice their faiths and build religious institutions. In fact, in big cities like Tehran a person can find a Muslim mosque, a Christian church, a Zoroastrian temple, and a Jewish synagogue on the same street.

Despite the law, followers of these religions often face discrimination. Many businesses and government agencies give priority to Muslim men when hiring or promoting workers, as do the universities. As Siyavash, a Zoroastrian teen, explains, "It is still difficult to get a good job. My uncle works in an office and is suitable for a manager, but they don't give the job because he is Zoroastrian."

Quoted in Nicholas Jubber, *Drinking Arak off an Ayatollah's Beard*. Philadelphia: Da Capo, 2010, p. 79.

tion secret. As Valli, a young homosexual male, explains, "If we get caught, they can kill us . . . it's not good. That is why we have to be secretive."[66]

It is not only strict laws that keep young homosexuals in the closet. Iranian culture views homosexuality very negatively. Known homosexuals are scorned by society and often by their families. Although they may want to open up to their loved ones, most do not out of fear of rejection. Author Ali Delforoush describes how his friend Siavash felt: "He wanted to tell his parents everything. . . . He wanted to scream that he was gay, that he was dying inside all the time and didn't want to hide it anymore. He wanted to be embraced by his parents for who he was. But he knew he could not."[67]

Young Iranians who do come out to their families frequently regret the decision. It is not unusual for parents to beat a homosexual child or cut off all ties with him or her. According to Hossein Alizadeh of the International Gay and Lesbian Human Rights Commission, "The number one threat to gays and lesbians in Iran is the family."[68]

In some cases young homosexuals are forced to enter into a heterosexual marriage by their families. Indeed, many homosexuals lead parallel lives. They are in heterosexual marriages while having secret same-sex affairs with prostitutes on the side.

Living a secret life takes its toll on these young people. Many report dealing with feelings of shame, frustration, and depression. Some flee the country. Others opt for sexual reassignment surgery, which is not only legal, but encouraged. The procedure is actually meant for transsexual individuals who do not identify with their birth gender and feel they were born the wrong sex. Although the surgery is performed on transsexual individuals in Iran, many of the patients are gay men and women who are not transsexual. These young people are usually not unhappy with their birth gender, but rather undergo the surgery because they cannot bear the hardship of living as a homosexual in Iran. Changing their gender allows them to be with whomever they prefer without persecution. As Valli explains, "Sometimes I think I should get a sex change. . . . That's what other guys did. A friend of mine, he wanted to be with his boyfriend so much he went to Mirjalali [a surgeon]."[69]

In fact, more sex reassignment surgeries are performed in Iran than anywhere else in the world except Thailand. These operations are subsidized by the government. "They want you to be one thing or the other," says Valli. "People like me, they encourage us to have sex change. . . . They even help you pay if you can't afford it."[70]

Critics say that the procedure is often forced on youngsters who have no issues with their gender identity and therefore do not need to have their gender changed to lead fulfilling lives. As Marie, a woman who had sexual reassignment surgery when she was a teenager, explains, "I think now if I were in a free society, I wonder if I would have been like I am now and if I would have changed my gender. I am not sure."[71] Still, access to the procedure gives some teens a way to reconcile their religion with their sexuality.

Important Holy Days

In addition to affecting Iranian teens' sexual lives, religion impacts when and how they hold celebrations. All Muslim holy days are observed in Iran. Among the most important is Ramadan. During this month-long holiday, Muslims from age twelve onward fast from sunrise to sunset in an effort to purify their souls. Although people go about daily tasks as usual, their food and drink intake is limited to a predawn breakfast and a post-sunset meal.

Fasting during Ramadan is compulsory. About one-third of Iranians get official exemptions from fasting due to health issues;

Young Iranian men study the Koran at a shrine during the month of Ramadan. The month is observed by fasting during daylight hours and focusing on spirituality.

however, anyone, even if officially exempt or a non-Muslim, is subject to punishment if caught eating or drinking in public during fasting hours. Many young Iranians believe that observing the fast should be a personal choice, not an obligation imposed on them by the government. Still, because people can lose their jobs or be expelled from a university for not fasting, many young people fast publicly, more to keep up appearances than out of religious devotion. According to Leyla, an Iranian woman, "Most Iranians . . . won't hesitate to eat heartily behind closed doors. What is important to them is the perception of others that they are fasting."[72]

Although some young Iranians observe Ramadan as a way to keep up appearances, they join with more devout teens to celebrate another Islamic holiday known as Eid al-Fitr. This two-day-long festival marks the end of Ramadan and is commemorated with family visits, gift giving, and large-scale communal

The Five Pillars of Islam

As soon as they are old enough to understand, almost all Iranian youngsters are taught to respect and follow the Five Pillars of Islam. These are five rules, or elements of faith, that all Muslims are expected to obey. The Five Pillars of Islam are the basic framework of daily life in Iran and serve as the basis for sharia law.

The first pillar requires that believers formally declare their faith. Muslims do this in their prayers by professing that there is only one God, Allah, and that Muhammad is his messenger. The second pillar requires that Muslims pray five times a day—at dawn, noon, afternoon, evening, and night. Time and space are allotted in Iranian schools, universities, and businesses so that everyone, young and old, can fulfill this requirement. The third pillar requires that Muslims give charity and help others. Acts of charity and helpfulness include not only financial assistance, but also the performance of kind deeds. It extends to family members, friends, neighbors, strangers, and the community at large. Iranian hospitality is one way young people fulfill this pillar. The fourth pillar requires that all Muslims fast during the holy month of Ramadan. The last pillar requires people to make at least one pilgrimage during their lifetime to the holy city of Mecca. Located in Saudi Arabia, Mecca is the birthplace of the Prophet Muhammad.

prayers. The holiday begins with huge public prayer sessions held in open-air areas throughout the nation. In Tehran the streets are closed to motor vehicles to make room for the enormous crowds that turn out for the occasion. Drawn by the merry atmosphere and the chance to come together and rejoice, the crowd includes people of all ages, political views, and devoutness, as well as vendors hawking balloons, beverages, and snacks. Indeed, for many young Iranians, attending the communal prayer session is a way to come together and honor their shared culture, no matter their political differences. As Madi Jahangir, the editor in chief of the website Dream of Iran, explains, "Iranians from every walk of life and social class, different appearance, children, men, women, old and young participate in Eid prayer. . . . After the start of prayer, the differences do not matter. What is seen . . . are thousands of people . . . practicing their religion so harmonically."[73] Clearly, whether in the form of joyful celebrations, solemn holidays, or state laws that enforce Islamic values, the Muslim religion plays a huge role in the lives of Iranian adolescents and teens.

SOURCE NOTES

Chapter One: A Complex Nation

1. Quoted in Ali Delforoush, *The Iranian Chronicles*. Blooming-ton, IN: iUniverse, 2012, p. 31.

2. Parsa, "Remembering Ourselves, Remembering Others," *Toptopic* (blog), November 26, 2016. https://toptopic.com.

3. Quoted in Nicholas Jubber, *Drinking Arak off an Ayatollah's Beard*. Philadelphia: Da Capo, 2010, p. 16.

4. Fatema, "Wednesday, June 15, 2005," *Iranian Girl* (blog), June 15, 2005. http://iranian-girl.blogspot.com.

5. Quoted in Roula Khalaf, "Iran's 'Generation Normal,'" *Financial Times*, May 29, 2015. www.ft.com.

6. Kaveh Basmenji, *Tehran Blues*. London: SAQI, 2005, p. 10.

7. Quoted in Channel 4, "Basij Militia Member's Story: Full Transcript," February 17, 2010. www.channel4.com.

8. Quoted in Basmenji, *Tehran Blues*, p. 25.

9. Quoted in Khalaf, "Iran's 'Generation Normal.'"

10. Jared Cohen, *Children of Jihad*. New York: Gotham, 2007, p. 36.

11. Quoted in Jubber, *Drinking Arak off an Ayatollah's Beard*, p. 19.

12. Quoted in Cohen, *Children of Jihad*, p. 81.

13. Quoted in Cohen, *Children of Jihad*, p. 42.

14. Quoted in Mike Krevar, "Tehran's Teens: Iran Isn't What You Think It Is," CNN, February 25, 2016. www.cnn.com.

Chapter Two: Home and Family

15. Quoted in Kamran Ashtary and Tori Egherman, "Growing Up in Iran," *View from Iran* (blog), August 27, 2006. http://viewfromiran.blogspot.com.

16. Quoted in Ann de Craemer, "The Big Lie," Tehran Review, May 4, 2010. http://tehranreview.net.

17. D.D., "The Ever Continuing Battle of Cultures! Please Read!," FarsiNet. http://farsinet.com.

18. Margaret Shaida, *The Legendary Cuisine of Persia*. New York: Interlink, 2001, p. 10.

19. Jamie Maslin, *Iranian Rappers and Persian Porn*. New York: Skyhorse, 2009, p. 135.

20. Jubber, *Drinking Arak off an Ayatollah's Beard*, p. 99.

21. Quoted in Mike Milotte, "Don't Skip Tehran's Unmissable Sights," Lonely Planet, 2017. www.lonelyplanet.com.

22. Jubber, *Drinking Arak off an Ayatollah's Beard*, p. 22.

23. Najmieh Batmanglij, *New Food of Life*. Washington, DC: Mage, 2005, p. 11.

24. Maslin, *Iranian Rappers and Persian Porn*, p. 58.

25. Maslin, *Iranian Rappers and Persian Porn*, p. 209.

Chapter Three: Education and Work

26. Shervin Malekzadeh, "Back to School in Iran: How to Deal with a Bad Summer," *Time*, September 7, 2009. http://content.time.com.

27. Malihe Maghazei, "Iran," in *Teen Life in the Middle East*, ed. Ali Akbar Mahdi. Westport, CT: Greenwood, 2003, p. 20.

28. Quoted in Ashtary and Egherman, "Growing Up in Iran."

29. Quoted in UNICEF, "Opening Up Education to Girls in Iran's Poorest Province," November 23, 2005. www.unicef.org.

30. Quoted in Fariba Sahraei, "Iranian University Bans on Women Causes Consternation," BBC News, September 22, 2012. www.bbc.com.

31. Quoted in Samira Hazari, "What Does School Education Look like in Iran?," British Council, April 21, 2015. www.britishcouncil.org.

32. Quoted in Cohen, *Children of Jihad*, p. 98.

33. Cohen, *Children of Jihad*, p. 32.

34. David Blair, "Iran's Big Woman Problem: All of the Things Iranian Women Aren't Allowed to Do," *Telegraph* (London), September 21, 2015. www.telegraph.co.uk.

35. Fatema, "Friday, October 28, 2005," *Iranian Girl* (blog), October 28, 2005. http://iranian-girl.blogspot.com.

36. Quoted in Nazanin Rafsanjani, "Iran Facing Dangerous Brain Drain," NPR, January 15, 2007. www.npr.org.

37. Quoted in Cohen, *Children of Jihad*, p. 36.

Chapter Four: Social Life

38. Quoted in Khalaf, "Iran's 'Generation Normal.'"

39. Quoted in Simon Worrall, "'To Live in Tehran You Have to Lie': Revealing Hidden Lives in Iran," National Geographic, September 7, 2014. http://news.nationalgeographic.com.

40. Jubber, *Drinking Arak off an Ayatollah's Beard*, p. 167.

41. Quoted in Cohen, *Children of Jihad*, p. 68.

42. Quoted in Jubber, *Drinking Arak off an Ayatollah's Beard*, p. 268.

43. Maslin, *Iranian Rappers and Persian Porn*, pp. 119–20.

44. Quoted in Catherine Bosley, "Iranian Erudition," *Varsity* (University of Cambridge, Cambridge, UK). www.varsity.co.uk.

45. Delforoush, *The Iranian Chronicles*, pp. 14–15.

46. Quoted in Christopher Thornton, "The Iran We Don't See: A Tour of the Country Where People Love Americans," *Atlantic*, June 6, 2012. www.theatlantic.com.

47. Khalaf, "Iran's 'Generation Normal.'"

48. Holly Dagres, "Instalran: How Instagram Managed to Seep Through the Cracks in Iran," *Huffington Post*, 2017. www.huffingtonpost.com.

49. Quoted in Cohen, *Children of Jihad*, p. 57.

50. Quoted in Bosley, "Iranian Erudition."

51. Quoted in Jessica Mudditt, "The Slippery Slope to Freedom in Iran," *Spiked*, April 17, 2009. www.spiked-online.com.

52. Quoted in Bill O'Driscoll, "Building a Movement," *Pittsburgh (PA) City Paper*, June 12, 2008. www.pghcitypaper.com.

53. Quoted in Sean Williams, "Meet the Parkour Women of Iran—Modern Feminism," Emirate Women, April 29, 2014. http://emirateswoman.com.

54. Quoted in Amy Braunschweiger, "Banned from Stadiums for Being a Woman in Iran," Human Rights Watch, June 30, 2016. www.hrw.org.

55. Quoted in Delforoush, *The Iranian Chronicles*, p. 10.

Chapter Five: Religious Influences

56. Quoted in Jubber, *Drinking Arak off an Ayatollah's Beard*, p. 32.

57. Quoted in Thomas Erdbrink, "Mr. Big Mouth," *New York Times* Videos: Life in Iran, *Iran Primer* (blog), US Institute of Peace, April 10, 2015. http://iranprimer.usip.org.

58. Cohen, *Children of Jihad*, p. 39.

59. Quoted in Ramita Navai, "High Heels and Hijabs: Iran's Sexual Revolution," *Statesman*, August 1, 2014. www.newstatesman.com.

60. Navai, "High Heels and Hijabs."

61. Quoted in Negar Farshidi, "Virginity Still a Commodity in Iran," Institute for War and Peace Reporting, February 4, 2011. https://iwpr.net.

62. Quoted in Farshidi, "Virginity Still a Commodity in Iran."

63. Quoted in Navai, "High Heels and Hijabs."

64. Quoted in Elaine Sciolino, "Love Finds a Way in Iran: Temporary Marriage," *New York Times*, October 4, 2000. http://collectiondevelopment.library.cornell.edu.

65. Quoted in *Iran Times* (Washington, DC), "Sex Can Be a Problem," October 18, 2013. http://iran-times.com.

66. Quoted in Jubber, *Drinking Arak off an Ayatollah's Beard*, p. 169.

67. Delforoush, *The Iranian Chronicles*, p. 112.

68. Quoted in Sune Engel Rasmussen, "Living Dangerously: What It's like to Be Gay in Iran," Vocativ, December 23, 2014. www.vocativ.com.

69. Quoted in Jubber, *Drinking Arak off an Ayatollah's Beard*, p. 169.

70. Quoted in Jubber, *Drinking Arak off an Ayatollah's Beard*, p. 169.

71. Quoted in Ali Hamedani, "The Gay People Pushed to Change Their Gender," BBC News, November 5, 2014. www.bbc.com.

72. Quoted in Maslin, *Iranian Rappers and Persian Porn*, p. 91.

73. Madi Jahangir, "Eid al Fitr in Iran: Practicing Religious Harmony," Dream of Iran, 2010. http://dreamofiran.com.

FOR FURTHER RESEARCH

Books

Noah Berlatsky, *The Iranian Revolution*. Farmington Hills, MI: Greenhaven, 2012.

William Mark Habeeb, *Major Nations of the Modern Middle East: Iran*. Broomall, PA: Mason Crest, 2015.

Herald McKinley, *Persia, the Rise of Islam, and the Holy Roman Empire*. New York: Gareth Stevens, 2015.

Jim Pipe, *Hoping for Peace in Iran*. New York: Gareth Stevens, 2012.

Vijeya Rajendra, *Iran*. New York: Cavendish Square, 2014.

Internet Sources

Central Intelligence Agency, "The World Factbook: Middle East: Iran," 2016. www.cia.gov/library/publications/resources/the-world-factbook/geos/ir.html.

Country Reports, "Iran Facts and Culture." www.countryreports.org/country/Iran.htm.

Fact Monster, "Iran." www.factmonster.com/country/iran.html.

Mick Krever, "Tehran's Teens: Iran Isn't What You Think It Is," CNN, February 25, 2016. www.cnn.com/2016/02/25/middleeast/iran-election-youth-tehran/index.html.

Karin Lehnardt, "60 Interesting Facts About Iran," Fact Retriever, November 2, 2016. www.factretriever.com/iran-facts.

Websites

Al-Monitor (www.al-monitor.com). This website provides articles related to Middle Eastern nations. It has a large section on Iran covering a wide range of topics.

Culture of Iran (www.cultureofiran.com). Culture of Iran offers articles and information about many aspects of life in Iran, including Iranian history, culture, food, and gender relations.

Iran Chamber Society (www.iranchamber.com). Iran Chamber Society has lots of articles related to Iran's history, art, and culture, as well as facts about the country.

Iran Primer (http://iranprimer.usip.org). This website provides a huge range of information covering all sorts of topics related to life in Iran.

Tehran Times (www.tehrantimes.com). The *Tehran Times* is Iran's leading international newspaper. All the articles relate to Iran and include everything from current events to sports. It also provides photos and videos.

INDEX

PICTURE CREDITS

Cover: iStockphoto.com

6: (top to bottom) fotosaga/Depositphotos.com
   iStockphoto.com/BornaMir
   Shutterstock.com/Henning Marquardt
   iStockphoto.com/ARSELA

9: iStockphoto.com/Leonid Andronov

13: nmessana/Depositphotos.com

17: iStockphoto.com/ajlber

21: Ahmad Halabisaz Xinhua News Agency/Newscom

26: Morteza Nikoubazl/SIPA/Newscom

28: iStockphoto.com/guenterguni

33: Associated Press

37: Associated Press

40: Siavash Habibollahi/ZUMA Press/Newscom

45: picture alliance/Jochen Eckel/Newscom

49: Associated Press

52: ALFRED/SIPA/Newscom

56: Associated Press

58: Associated Press

63: Associated Press

ABOUT THE AUTHOR

Barbara Sheen is the author of ninety-six nonfiction books for young people. She lives in New Mexico with her family. In her spare time she likes to swim, garden, cook, and walk.